Exploring
North America
Continents of the World
Geography Series

Author: Michael Kramme, Ph.D.

Consultants: Schyrlet Cameron and Carolyn Craig

Editors: Mary Dieterich and Sarah M. Anderson

COPYRIGHT 2012 Mark Twain Media, Inc.

ISBN 978-1-58037-631-0

Printing No. CD-404175

Mark Twain Media, Inc., Publishers
Distributed by Carson-Dellosa Publishing LLC

Map Source: Mountain High Maps® Copyright © 1997 Digital Wisdom, Inc.

Visit us at www.carsondellosa.com

Table of Contents

Introduction to the Teacher 1

The Continents
Close-Up 2
Knowledge Check 4
Map Follow-Up 5
Explore 6

The Continent of North America
Close-Up 7
Outline Map of North America 8
Knowledge Check 9
Map Follow-Up 10

North America's Climate
Close-Up 11
Knowledge Check 12
Map Follow-Up 13

North America's Resources and Industries
Close-Up 14
Knowledge Check 15
Map Follow-Up 16

North America's Animal Life
Close-Up 17
Knowledge Check 18
Explore 19

The Native People of North America
Close-Up 20
Knowledge Check 21
Map Follow-Up 22

The People of North America
Close-Up 23
Knowledge Check 24
Explore 25

Canada
Close-Up 26
Knowledge Check 27
Map Follow-Up 28

The United States
Close-Up 29
Knowledge Check 30
Map Follow-Up 31
Map Follow-Up 32

Mexico
Close-Up 33
Knowledge Check 34
Map Follow-Up 35

Central America
Close-Up 36
Knowledge Check 37
Map Follow-Up 38

North America's Islands
Close-Up 39
Knowledge Check 41
Map Follow-Up 42

Glossary 43

Bibliography 44

Answer Keys 45

Photo Credits C3

Introduction to the Teacher

Exploring North America is one of the seven books in Mark Twain Media's *Continents of the World Geography Series.* This series can be used to supplement the middle-school geography and social studies curriculum. The books support the goal of the National Geography Standards to prepare students for life in a global community by strengthening geographical literacy.

The intent of the *Continents of the World Geography Series* is to help students better understand the world around them through the study of geography. Each book focuses on one continent. Information and facts are presented in an easy-to-read and easy-to-understand format that does not overwhelm the learner. The text presents only the most important information in small, organized bites to make it easier for students to comprehend. Vocabulary words are boldfaced in the text. For quick reference, these words are listed in a glossary at the back of the book.

The series is specifically designed to facilitate planning for the diverse learning styles and skill levels of middle-school students. Each book is divided into several units. Each unit provides the teacher with alternative methods of instruction.

Unit Features
- Close-Up introduces facts and information as a reading exercise.
- Knowledge Check assesses student understanding of the reading exercise using selected response and constructed response questioning strategies.
- Map Follow-Up provides opportunities for students to report information from a spatial perspective.
- Explore allows students to expand learning by participating in high-interest, hands-on activities.
- Glossary lists the boldfaced words with definitions.

Online Resources
- Reluctant Reader Text: A modified version of the reading exercise pages can be downloaded from the website at www.carsondellosa.com. In the Search box, enter the product code CD-404175. When you reach the *Exploring North America* product page, click the icon for the Reluctant Reader Text download.
- The readability level of the text has been modified to facilitate struggling readers. The Flesch-Kincaid Readability formula, which is built into Microsoft® Word™ was used to determine the readability level. The formula calculates the number of words, sentences, and paragraphs in each selection to produce a reading level.

Additional Resources
Classroom Decoratives: The *Seven Continents of the World* and *World Landmarks and Locales Topper* bulletin board sets are available through Mark Twain Media/Carson-Dellosa Publishing LLC. These classroom decoratives visually reinforce geography lessons found in the *Continents of the World Geography Series* in an interesting and attention-grabbing way.

The Continents: Close-Up

A **continent** is a large landmass completely or mostly surrounded by water. The continents make up just over 29 percent of the earth's surface. They occupy about 57,100,000 square miles (148,000,000 sq. km). More than 65 percent of the land area is in the Northern Hemisphere.

The Continents Today

Landmasses

- Continents: Geographers list North America, South America, Europe, Asia, Africa, Australia, and Antarctica as continents.
- Subcontinents: Greenland and the India-Pakistan area are sometimes referred to as "subcontinents."
- Microcontinents: Madagascar and the Seychelles Islands are often called "microcontinents."
- Oceania: The island groups in the Pacific Ocean are called Oceania, but they are not considered a continent.

How Were the Continents Formed?

For many years, Europeans believed the continents were formed by a catastrophe or series of catastrophes, such as floods, earthquakes, and volcanoes. In 1596, a Dutch mapmaker, Abraham Ortelius, noted that the Americas' eastern coasts and the western coasts of Europe and Africa looked as if they fit together. He proposed that once they had been joined but later were torn apart.

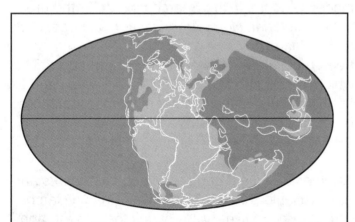

Wegener's theoretical continent, Pangaea, during the Permian Age (white outlines indicate current continents)

Many years later, a German named Alfred Lothar Wegener published a book in which he explained his theory of the "**Continental Drift**." Wegener, like Ortelius, believed that the earth originally had one supercontinent. He named it **Pangaea** from the Greek word meaning "all lands." He believed that the large landmass was a lighter rock that floated on a heavier rock, like ice floats on water.

Wegener's theory stated that the landmasses were still moving at a rate of about one yard each century. Wegener believed that Pangaea existed in the Permian Age. Then Pangaea slowly divided into two continents,

2

the upper part, **Laurasia**, and the lower, **Gondwanaland**, during the Triassic Age.

By the Jurassic Age, the landmasses had moved into what we could recognize as the seven continents, although they were still located near each other. Eventually, the continents "drifted" to their present locations.

Most scientists had been in agreement on the continental drift theory until researchers in the 1960s discovered several major mountain ranges on the ocean floor.

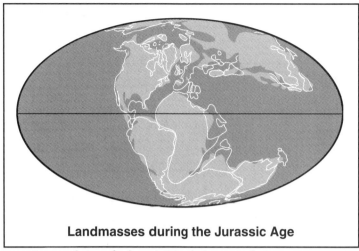

Landmasses during the Jurassic Age

These mountains suggested that the earth's crust consists of about 20 slabs or **plates**.

These discoveries led to a new theory, "**Plate Tectonics**," which has become more popular. This theory suggests that these plates move a few inches each year. In some places the plates are moving apart, while in others, the plates are colliding or scraping against each other.

Scientists also discovered that most volcanoes and earthquakes occur along the boundaries of the various plates. Recent earthquakes near Indonesia and Japan along the boundaries of the Indo-Australian, Eurasian, Philippine, and Pacific Plates have triggered devastating tsunamis that killed hundreds of thousands of people. Scientists hope that further study will help them increase their understanding of Earth's story.

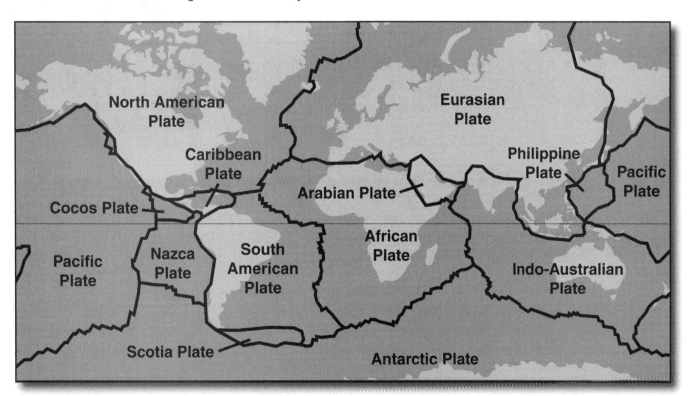

The earth's crust consists of about 20 plates. Plate tectonics suggest that these plates move a few inches each year.

Name: _____ Date: _____

Knowledge Check

Matching

_____ 1. Plate Tectonics
_____ 2. Laurasia
_____ 3. continent
_____ 4. Gondwanaland
_____ 5. Pangaea

a. lower part of Pangaea
b. Greek word meaning "all lands"
c. theory suggesting that plates move a few inches each year
d. upper part of Pangaea
e. a large landmass completely or mostly surrounded by water

Multiple Choice

6. He explained his theory of the Continental Drift.

   a. Abraham Ortelius
   b. Alfred Lothar Wegener
   c. Pangaea
   d. Laurasia

7. The earth's crust consists of _____ plates.

   a. about 20
   b. about 10
   c. about 5
   d. about 50

Did You Know?

Earth is thought to be the only planet in our solar system that has plate tectonics.

Constructed Response

Explain how the movement of the earth's plates formed the seven continents. Use two details from the selection to support your answer.

_____
_____
_____
_____
_____
_____

Name: _____ Date: _____

Map Follow-Up

Directions: There are seven continents and four oceans. Match the numbers on the map with the names of the continents and oceans.

_____ Pacific Ocean   _____ Arctic Ocean   _____ Atlantic Ocean

_____ Indian Ocean   _____ Africa   _____ Antarctica

_____ Asia   _____ Australia   _____ Europe

_____ North America   _____ South America

Continents and Oceans

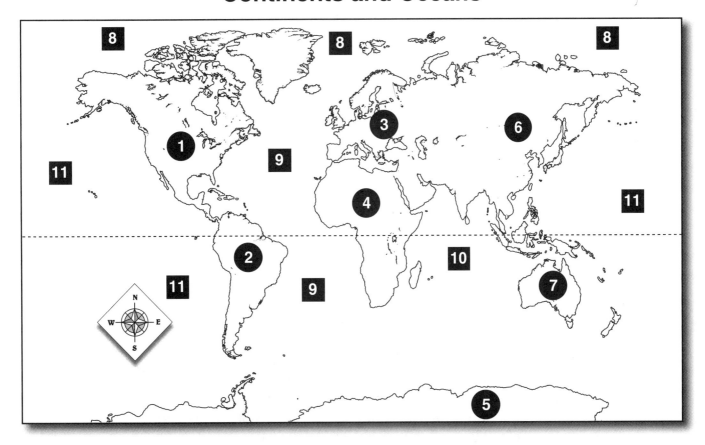

Name: _____   Date: _____

Explore: Papier-Mâché Globe

Materials

9 inch balloon	1 cup Elmer's glue	spray paint
empty coffee can	1 cup water	plastic container
newspaper	scissors	wooden spoon
blue and green tissue paper	blank world map	2 paper plates
12" x 12" cardboard sheet	cardboard toilet tissue roll	straight pin

Directions

Day 1

Step 1: Mix 1 cup Elmer's glue with 1 cup water in a plastic container.

Step 2: Cover work area with newspaper. Blow up the balloon and tie. Place balloon, knot side down in the coffee can.

Step 3: Tear newspapers into 1" strips. Dip strips into the glue and run the strip through your fingers to remove excess. Place the wet strip of newspaper across the balloon and smooth it down until it sticks. Add strips until the entire balloon is covered. Add two more layers. Allow the balloon to dry overnight.

Day 2

Step 1: Turn the balloon over so that the tied end is up. Use a pin to pop the balloon. Remove the balloon. Now you have a blank globe.

Step 2: Print out a blank world map to use as a stencil. Use scissors to cut out the landmasses and trace around them onto the globe.

Step 3: Tear blue tissue paper into small squares, dip in glue, and cover the ocean area.

Step 4: Tear green tissue paper into small squares, dip in glue and cover the landmass areas of the globe.

Step 5: Allow the globe to dry over night.

Day 3

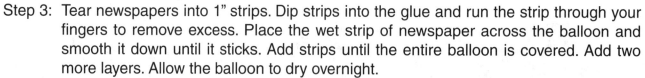

Step 1: To make the globe stand, glue 2 paper plates together. Cut cardboard into five 4" squares. With paper plates right side up, glue one square of cardboard to the middle of the plate. Glue another on top of that slightly offset. Continue layering and gluing for all 5 squares. Cut slits in one end of the toilet tissue roll 1" up and 1" apart. Fold these outward making flaps. With paper plates bottom up, glue the flaps and place and press in the center of the plate. Let dry.

Sept 2: Spray paint the cardboard tube and paper plate and allow to dry.

Sept 3: When dry, insert the tube into the hole at the bottom of the globe. Adjust to make the globe stand straight.

The Continent of North America: Close-Up

North America is the third largest of the seven continents. It includes Canada, the United States, Mexico, Greenland, the countries of Central America, and the West Indies Islands. North America covers over 9,200,000 square miles (23,800,000 sq. km). Together with South America, North America forms the land in what is known as the **Western Hemisphere**.

North America is bordered on the east by the Atlantic Ocean, on the west by the Pacific Ocean, on the north by the Arctic Ocean and on the south by the Gulf of Mexico. It is separated from South America by the border between Panama and Colombia. Some geographers claim that the **Isthmus of Panama** actually divides the two continents.

The continent's lowest point is Death Valley, California. It is 282 feet (86 m) below sea level. The highest point is Mount McKinley in Alaska. It is 20,320 feet (6,194 m) above sea level.

Major Regions

- The **Canadian Shield** includes eastern Canada, most of Greenland, and part of the northern United States. Part of the region is frozen wasteland, and other parts contain poor soil and large forests.

- A **coastal plain** covers most of the eastern United States and Mexico.

- The third region is a narrow strip that contains many hills and the Appalachian Mountains of the United States.

- The fourth region includes the **central plain** extending from southern Canada to Texas known as the Great Plains. This region includes most of the continent's agricultural lands. It is mainly flat land, but has some hilly regions.

- The fifth region is the western part of the continent and includes the western United States and Canada and most of Mexico. This region includes the Rocky Mountains of the United States and Canada and the Sierra Madres of southern California and Mexico.

Major River Systems and Lakes

- The Great Lakes and St. Lawrence River drain into the northern Atlantic Ocean. The Mississippi and Missouri Rivers drain most of the central United States and part of southern Canada into the Gulf of Mexico. The Mackenzie River, which flows into the Arctic Ocean, drains much of western Canada.

- Most of North America's lakes are in the northern part of the continent. Lake Superior is the world's largest freshwater lake. Other major lakes include the remainder of the Great Lakes: Erie, Huron, Michigan, and Ontario, as well as Lake Mead on the Colorado River, and the Great Salt Lake in Utah.

Name: _____ Date: _____

Outline Map of North America

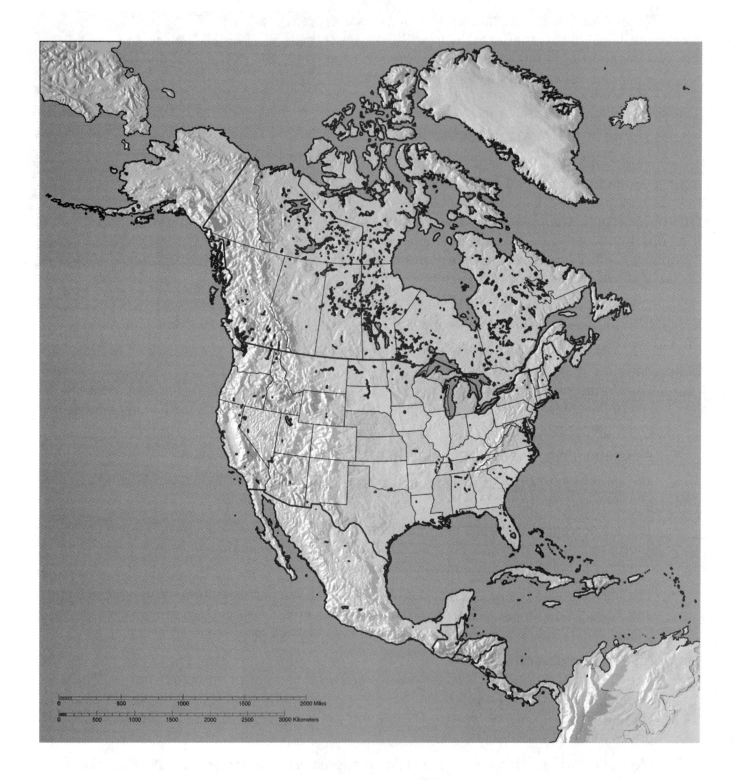

Name: _____   Date: _____

Knowledge Check

Matching

_____ 1. Isthmus of Panama   a. South America and North America form this

_____ 2. Canadian Shield   b. divides North and South America

_____ 3. coastal plain   c. includes eastern Canada, most of Greenland, and

_____ 4. Western   part of the northern United States

        Hemisphere   d. covers most of the eastern United States and Mexico

_____ 5. central plain   e. extends from southern Canada to Texas

Multiple Choice

6. This is the world's largest freshwater lake.

   a. Lake Mead
   b. Great Salt Lake
   c. Lake Superior
   d. Lake Michigan

7. This region includes most of the continent's agricultural lands.

   a. coastal plain
   b. Canadian Shield
   c. Death Valley
   d. Great Plains

Did You Know?

North America covers just over 16 percent of the world's surface, yet has only about eight percent of the world's population.

Constructed Response

Describe the difference between the coastal plain region of the North American continent and the central plain region. Use details from the reading selection to support your answer.

_____

_____

_____

_____

_____

_____

_____

Name: _____   Date: _____

Map Follow-Up

Directions: Match the names listed below with the numbers on the map. Also label the Atlantic Ocean, Pacific Ocean, Arctic Ocean, Gulf of Mexico, and Caribbean Sea.

_____ Canada   _____ Central America   _____ Greenland

_____ West Indies Islands _____ United States   _____ Mexico

North America

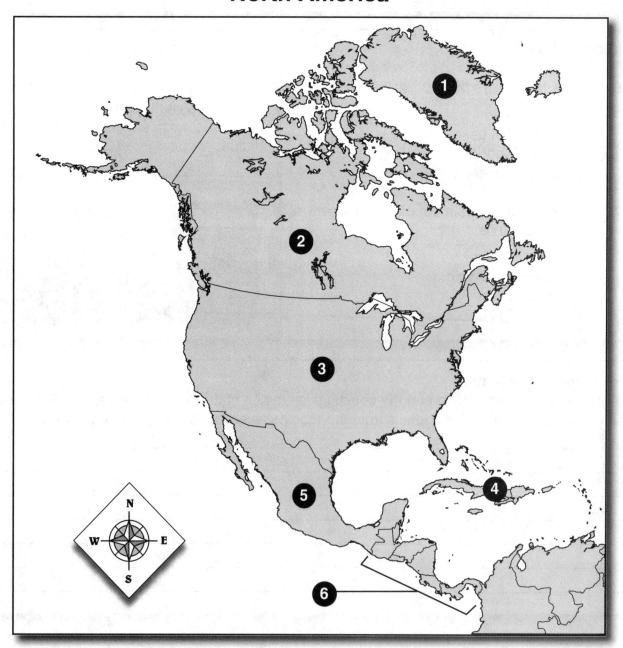

North America's Climate: Close-Up

North America has the full range of climate types, ranging from arctic in the far north to tropical in the south.

- Alaska, Greenland, and northern Canada have **arctic** and **subarctic climates**. The region is covered with snow and ice during all or most of the year. The winters are bitterly cold with long nights and short days. The southern part of this region has short, mild summers, while the northern part includes vast amounts of tundra.

- **Humid continental climate** regions of North America include some of southern Canada and the northeast fourth of the United States. The humid continental climate includes cold winters and hot summers, with adequate amounts of precipitation.

- The southeastern part of the United States is in a **humid subtropical climate** zone. Here, the winters are often warm, and the summers are hot and humid.

Ice Cap
Tundra
Subarctic
Desert
Tropical Savanna
Tropical Rain Forest
Humid Continental, Cool Summer
Undifferentiated Highlands
Humid Continental, Warm Summer
Mediterranean
Marine West Coast

North American climate map

- The northwestern part of the United States and the southwest corner of Canada have a **highland climate**. This is the climate in the mountain regions. This region has mild winters and warm summers. It also has significant amounts of precipitation.

- Most of the western United States experiences **semi-desert** and **desert climates**. These regions have hot daytime temperatures with cool nights and very little rainfall.

- The west coast of the United States includes both **marine west coast** and **Mediterranean climates**. These regions have moderate temperatures and adequate rainfall.

- **Mexico's climate zones** include desert and semi-desert regions as well as some highland and tropical areas. Rainfall amounts in these regions vary, but the winters are usually mild, and the summers are hot.

- Parts of southern Mexico and most of Central America are in a **tropical climate** zone. This climate features hot temperatures and much rainfall throughout the year. Tropical rain forests are common in the Central American countries

Name: _____ Date: _____

Knowledge Check

Matching

_____ 1. semi-desert
_____ 2. highland climate
_____ 3. tropical climate
_____ 4. humid continental climate
_____ 5. Mediterranean climate

a. features hot temperatures and much rainfall throughout the year
b. these regions have hot daytime temperatures with cool nights and very little rainfall
c. this region has mild winters and warm summers
d. this region has moderate temperatures and adequate rainfall
e. includes cold winters and hot summers, with adequate amounts of precipitation

Multiple Choice

6. The southeastern part of the United States has

   a. humid subtropical climate.
   b. humid continental climate.
   c. highland climate.
   d. subarctic climate.

7. Parts of southern Mexico and most of Central America are in this climate zone.

   a. highland
   b. arctic
   c. semi-desert
   d. tropical

Did You Know?

About 81% of Greenland is covered by a layer of ice. The ice has an average depth of about 5,000 feet (1,500 m). However, in recent years, the ice has been melting at an increased rate.

Constructed Response

Describe the climate zone of your state, province, or region. Give details to support your answer.

_____

_____

_____

_____

_____

_____

Name: _____ Date: _____

Map Follow-Up

Directions: Complete the climate map of North America. Locate and color each of the climate regions on the map. Fill in the Map Key with the colors you used on the map.

Climate Map of North America

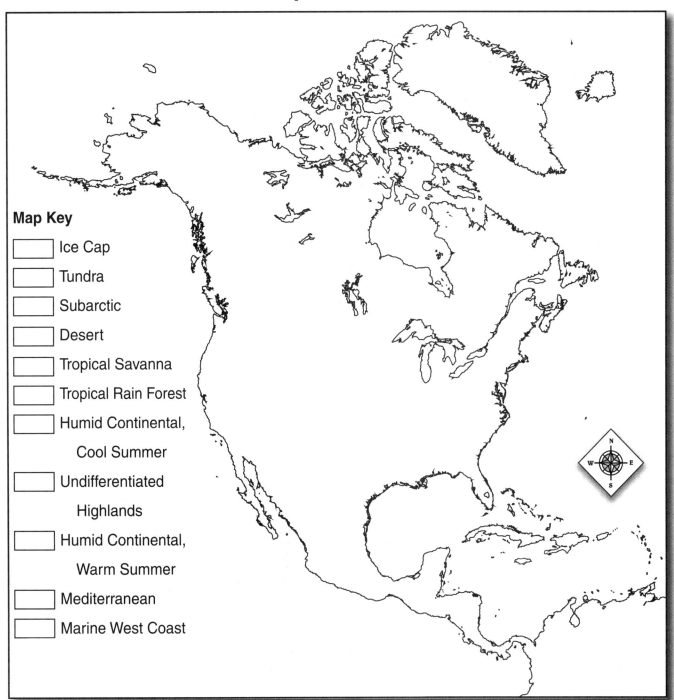

Map Key

☐ Ice Cap

☐ Tundra

☐ Subarctic

☐ Desert

☐ Tropical Savanna

☐ Tropical Rain Forest

☐ Humid Continental, Cool Summer

☐ Undifferentiated Highlands

☐ Humid Continental, Warm Summer

☐ Mediterranean

☐ Marine West Coast

North America's Resources and Industries: Close-Up

North America has a wide variety of industries and valuable natural resources.

Natural Resources

Large deposits of **petroleum** and natural gas are in Alaska, western Canada, the southwestern United States, and eastern Mexico. Proposals for new drilling in Alaska and the Gulf of Mexico have continued to bring protests from environmentalists. Even with its large deposits, the United States **imports** a large amount of petroleum each year.

Coal is mined in large quantities in the United States and Canada. Great amounts of iron ore come from the United States, Canada, and Mexico. Other plentiful minerals include copper, lead, nickel, sulfur, uranium, and zinc. Gold and silver are also mined throughout the continent.

Industries

North America has a wide range of industries. Both Canada and the United States are highly industrialized. Mexico and the Central American countries are less developed, but they are becoming more industrialized. Major industries include electronics, food and beverage processing, chemicals, forest and paper products, machinery, motor vehicles, clothing, and textiles.

- **Agriculture** is a major industry throughout much of the continent. It is highly mechanized in Canada and the United States. In Mexico and Central America, much of the agriculture is labor-intensive. About three percent of the population in Canada and two percent in the United States work at farming, while in Mexico, the farming population is about 23 percent.

  Grains and livestock are raised on the plains of Canada and the United States. California, Florida, and Texas are notable producers of fruits and vegetables. Other agricultural products include cotton, dairy products, and sugar cane.

- **Forestry** is a major industry in Canada and the western United States.

- **Fishing** is the most important industry in Greenland. Fishing is also done along the entire coast of the continent.

  Canada, the United States, and Mexico **consume** enormous amounts of energy. A combination of nuclear, hydroelectric, wind, solar, geothermal, coal, petroleum, and natural gas is necessary to supply the ever-increasing demand.

Major **exports** of the United States include food, chemicals, machinery, and transportation vehicles. Canada's major exports include chemicals, forest products, food, and metals. Mexico's major export is **crude oil**. Mexico and the Central American countries also export coffee and minerals.

Name: _____ Date: _____

Knowledge Check

Matching

_____ 1. fishing   a. a major industry in Canada and the western United States

_____ 2. coal   b. a major industry throughout much of North America

_____ 3. forestry   c. Mexico's major export

_____ 4. crude oil   d. mined in large quantities in the United States and Canada

_____ 5. agriculture   e. most important industry in Greenland

Multiple Choice

6. What percent of the population in Canada and the United States work at farming?

   a. 23 and 25 percent
   b. 10 and 9 percent
   c. 3 and 2 percent
   d. 30 and 40 percent

7. Which state is NOT a notable producer of fruits and vegetables?

   a. California
   b. Texas
   c. Florida
   d. Maine

Did You Know?

Corn was not known in Europe until Christopher Columbus brought some back from his first voyage to North America.

Constructed Response

Explain why it is important for a nation to have an abundance of natural resources. Use details from the reading selection to support your answer.

_____

_____

_____

_____

_____

_____

Name: _____   Date: _____

Map Follow-Up

Directions: Complete the map below. Create a symbol for each of the products and natural resources listed in the Map Key. Draw the symbol in the Map Key. Add the symbol to the blank map to show the regions in North America that are a major source of the product or natural resource.

Resources and Products of North America

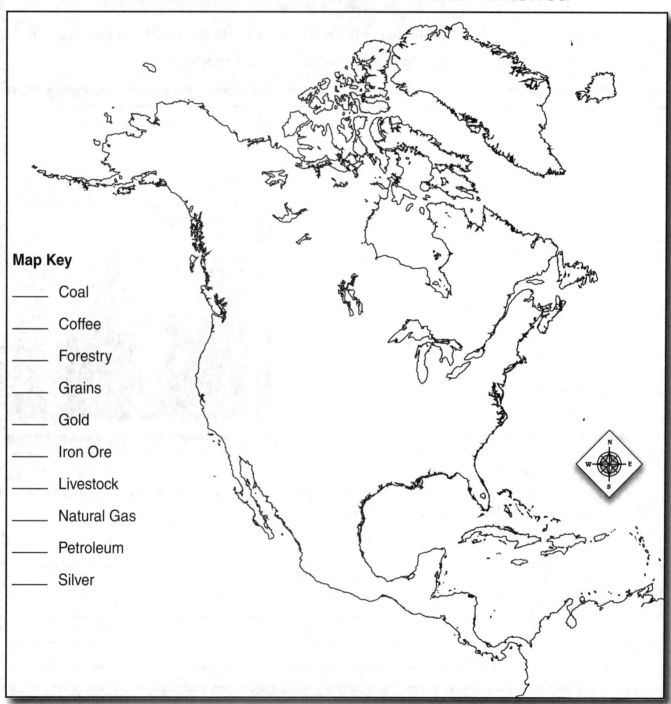

Map Key

_____ Coal

_____ Coffee

_____ Forestry

_____ Grains

_____ Gold

_____ Iron Ore

_____ Livestock

_____ Natural Gas

_____ Petroleum

_____ Silver

North America's Animal Life: Close-Up

North America has a large variety of animal species.

Mammals:

- In addition to **domesticated** animals such as dogs, cats, horses, and livestock, many wild mammals live on the continent.
- Common mammals include the bat, beaver, coyote, fox, opossum, porcupine, raccoon, wolf, and a variety of rodents. The plains and prairies are home to antelope and deer as well as burrowing animals such as gophers and prairie dogs.
- Larger mammals include bison, caribou, moose, deer, jaguar, oxen, puma, and sheep. Bison are either raised in protected environments or as livestock. Several varieties of bear also live in the northern regions. The world's largest bears include the grizzly bear and the polar bear.

Reptiles:

- Poisonous snakes include the cottonmouth, rattlesnake, and copperhead.
- Other reptiles include a variety of nonpoisonous snakes and lizards (including chameleons). Gila monsters and beaded lizards are the world's only poisonous lizards. The beaded lizard lives in Mexico. The Gila monster is found in the southwestern United States.

Water Animals:

- North America's rivers and lakes are home to many species of freshwater fish. A variety of shellfish and finfish live in the coastal regions.
- Larger coastal inhabitants include whales, dolphins, and sharks.

Birds:

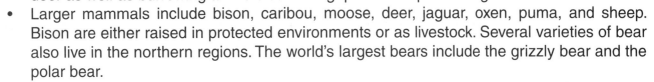

- The continent is also the **habitat** of over 800 species of birds. The variety of birds ranges from the tiny hummingbird to the large California condor.
- North America also provides a haven for a variety of marsh and inland water birds, including herons, ducks, pelicans, and geese. Birds of prey that live in North America include many species of eagles, hawks, and falcons.
- The Central America region is home to many colorful tropical varieties of birds.

The natural habitats of most animals were **decreased** as humans settled in more of the continent. The loss of habitats, increased pollution, and the use of **pesticides** have continued to decrease the total number of animals living on the continent. The passenger pigeon, Carolina parakeet, and heath hen all became **extinct**. The bison, whooping crane, bald eagle, and wild turkey came close to extinction. Through the efforts of **conservationists**, these species are slowly increasing in number.

Name: _____ Date: _____

Knowledge Check

Matching

_____ 1. marsh and inland water birds

_____ 2. common mammals

_____ 3. poisonous snakes

_____ 4. beaded lizard

_____ 5. domesticated animals

a. one of the world's only poisonous lizards

b. cottonmouth, rattlesnake, and copperhead

c. dogs, cats, horses, and livestock

d. bat, beaver, coyote, fox, opossum, porcupine, raccoon, and wolf

e. herons, ducks, pelicans, and geese

Multiple Choice

6. Which of the following birds is NOT extinct?

    a. whooping crane
    b. passenger pigeon
    c. Carolina parakeet
    d. heath hen

7. What has contributed to the slow increase in the numbers of certain endangered animal species on the North American continent?

    a. loss of habitats
    b. increased pollution
    c. use of pesticides
    d. conservationists

Did You Know?

The whooping crane almost became extinct. In 1939, only 18 were left in the world. Efforts by conservationists have slowly increased their numbers.

Constructed Response

What has contributed to the decrease in the total number of animals living on the continent of North America? Explain, using details from the reading selection to support your answer.

_____

_____

_____

_____

_____

_____

_____

Name: _____ Date: _____

Explore: Animal Postcard

Directions: Create a North American animal postcard. First, research one of the animals from the reading selection. Then, draw a picture of this animal on the front of your postcard. On the back of the card, in the upper left-hand side, write a sentence telling about your animal. On the back of the card, in the lower left-hand side, write three facts about your animal. Now, write an address on the right-hand side of the back of the card. Draw a stamp in the space where the stamp should go. Cut the postcard out along the lines. Fold the postcard in half and tape or glue the sides together.

Front of Postcard: Draw picture

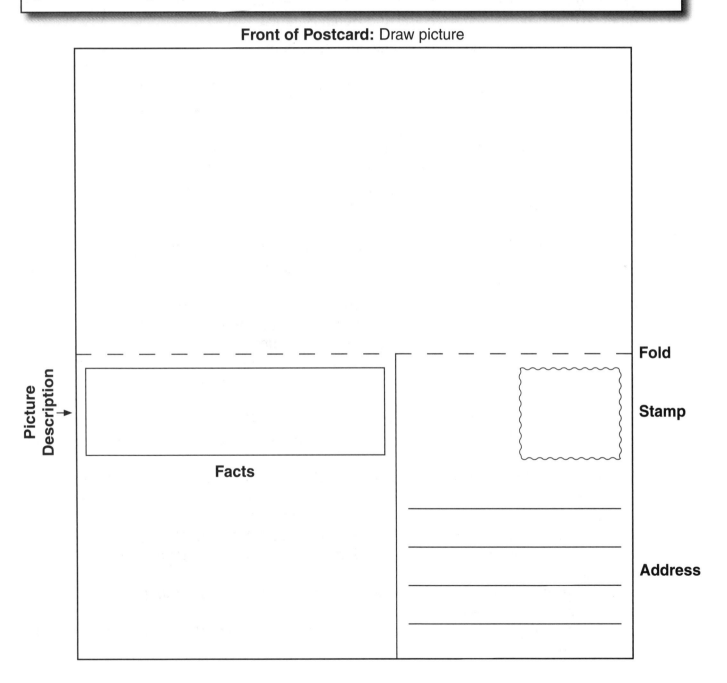

Fold

Picture Description →

Stamp

Facts

Address

The Native People of North America: Close-Up

When the first Europeans came to North America, many tribes of people, who later became known as Indians, lived throughout the continent. Anthropologists believe that these people were descended from the people of northeast Asia. It is commonly believed that, approximately 20,000 to 30,000 years ago, hunters looking for new hunting grounds crossed a land bridge that connected Asia and North America. The land bridge, which no longer exists, was near what is now the Bering Strait. These early hunters continued to move south into the rest of North America and eventually into Central and South America.

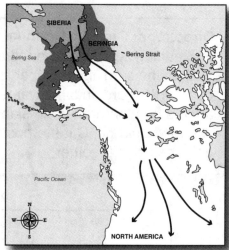

The Native American tribes are divided into several major cultural groups.

1. The native inhabitants of the northern arctic and subarctic regions are also known as **Northern Hunters**. They include the Aleuts, Chipewyan, and Inuit (known as Eskimo). They are hunters of caribou, polar bear, walrus, seal, and whale.

2. The **Woodland group** inhabited the eastern part of the continent. They grew crops and used wood for housing, weapons, utensils, and canoes. Major woodland tribes included the Algonquian-speaking tribes of Delaware, Chippewa, Massachusett, Micmac, and Pequot. The Iroquois-speaking woodland tribes included the Cayuga, Mohawk, Oneida, Onondaga, and Seneca.

3. The **Plains tribes** lived in the west central region. They relied on hunting herds of bison, deer, elk, and antelope. Plains tribes included the Arapaho, Blackfoot, Cheyenne, Comanche, Crow, Osage, Pawnee, Sioux, and Wichita.

4. **Pueblo tribes** lived in the southwestern United States and northern Mexico. They lived in houses made of adobe, which is a sun-dried clay brick. *Pueblo* is Spanish for "village." Pueblo tribes included the Apache, Hopi, Navajo, Yuma, and Zuni.

5. The **Pacific Northwest tribes** included the Chinook, Haida, Kwakiutl, Nootka, and Tlingit. The men were hunters and fishers, and the women gathered seeds, berries, and nuts for food.

6. The **California tribes** of Chumash, Karok, Maidu, Miwok, Pomo, and Yahi are also known as "seed gatherers of the desert." Their diets include berries, nuts, seeds, and roots. They are known for their basket weavers.

7. The **Great Basin tribes** of the Ute, Paiute, and Shoshone and the **Plateau tribes** of the Nez Perce, Spokane, and Yakima lived in the western region of what is now the United States and Canada between the Rocky Mountains and the coastal ranges.

8. The **Southeast tribes** of Alabama, Atakapa, Caddo, Catawba, Cherokee, Chickasaw, Choctaw, Natchez, Seminole, and Ticucua lived in what is now the southern and southeastern United States.

9. **Mexican tribes** included the Coahujltec, Concho, Lagunero, Seri, Yaqui, and the ancient Aztecs, Olmecs, and Toltecs.

10. **Central American tribes** included the Mixtec, Tarascan, and Zapotec, as well as the ancient Mayan culture.

Name: _____   Date: _____

Knowledge Check

Matching

_____ 1. Northern Hunters

_____ 2. Plains tribes

_____ 3. Woodland group

_____ 4. Southeast tribes

_____ 5. Pueblo tribes

a. inhabited the eastern part of the continent

b. lived in what is now the southern and southeastern United States

c. native inhabitants of the northern arctic and subarctic regions

d. lived in the southwestern United States and northern Mexico

e. lived in the west central region

Multiple Choice

6. The Apache are members of the

   a. Southeast tribe.

   b. Mexican tribe.

   c. Pueblo tribe.

   d. California tribe.

7. The Flathead and Nez Perce are members of the

   a. Pacific Northwest tribe.

   b. Great Basin and Plateau tribes.

   c. Pueblo tribes.

   d. Northern Hunters.

Did You Know?

Twenty five states of the United States have names derived from Native American languages.

Constructed Response

Anthropologists believe the first inhabitants of North America came from Asia. Explain how this might have happened, using details from the reading selection to support your answer.

_____

_____

_____

_____

_____

_____

_____

Name: _____ Date: _____

Map Follow-Up

Directions: Match the numbers on the map with the major Native American culture groups listed below. Use the reading selection and the names of the tribes listed on the map to help you.

_____ California   _____ Great Basin   _____ Northern Hunters

_____ Pueblo   _____ Pacific Northwest   _____ Plains

_____ Southeast   _____ Woodland   _____ Plateau

Native American Culture Groups

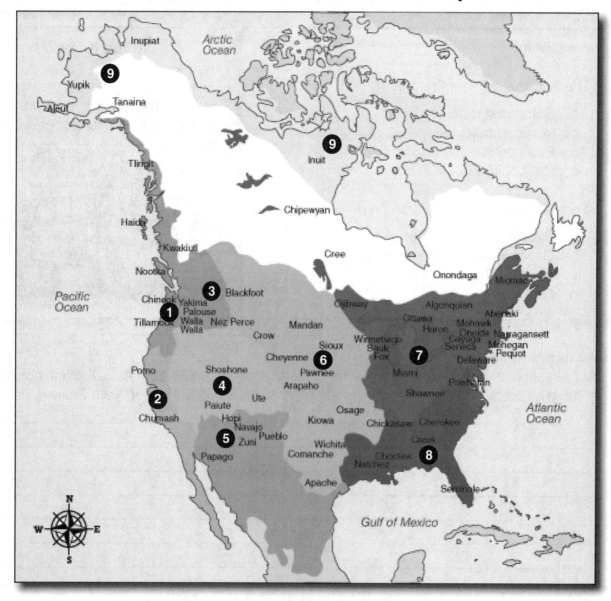

The People of North America: Close-Up

Long before the arrival of European settlers, North America had a diverse group of **indigenous** people. An indigenous person is one who originally inhabited a certain location. North America's indigenous people were referred to as "Indians" for many years. The term Indian has its origin from Christopher Columbus, who upon landing in the Americas thought he was in the East Indies islands. Today, the preferred term is "Native American."

Population

Today's population of North America is mostly of European descent. Over 35 percent of Canada's population is descended from the British Isles. About 16 percent is descended from the French. A large number of Canada's population is also of other European descent.

The United States' population is more diverse than Canada's. About 30 percent of America's people have a British or Irish heritage. Those of German and Scandinavian descent make up about 21 percent of the population. African Americans make up about 12.6 percent, Hispanics about 16.3 percent, and those of Asian ancestry make up about 4.8 percent of the people of the United States. Native Americans make up about 0.9 percent of the population.

Approximately 60 percent of the people of Mexico and Central America are mestizos. A *mestizo* is a person of mixed Native American and European (mostly Spanish) descent. It is estimated that about 30 percent of Mexican and Central American people are of pure Native American **ancestry** and about ten percent of pure European descent.

About 75 percent of North America's people live in **urban** areas. **Mexico City** and New York City are among the top 20 largest cities in the world.

Language

English is the **primary** language in the United States and most of Canada. French is the main language of about one-third of Canadians. Spanish is the primary language of Mexico and Central America. Several Native American groups, including the Navajo and the Inuit (Eskimo), speak their native languages.

Religion

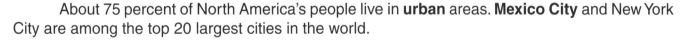

Christianity is the principal religion of North America. The great **majority** of Mexican and Central Americans, approximately 43 percent of Canadians, and 25 percent of U.S. **inhabitants** are Roman Catholic. Protestants make up about 50 percent of the population. The United States and Canada also have large communities of Jews and Eastern Orthodox Christians. The number of Muslims in North America is also increasing.

Name: _____ Date: _____

Knowledge Check

Matching

_____ 1. mestizo

_____ 2. indigenous

_____ 3. English

_____ 4. Mexico City

_____ 5. Christianity

a. one of the world's largest cities

b. the principal religion of North America

c. a person of mixed Native American and European (mostly Spanish) descent

d. one who originally inhabited a certain location

e. primary language in the United States and most of Canada

Multiple Choice

6. What percent of North America's people live in urban areas?

    a. 50 percent
    b. 75 percent
    c. 95 percent
    d. 30 percent

7. This is the main language of about one-third of Canadians.

    a. English
    b. German
    c. French
    d. Spanish

Did You Know?

Many historians believe that the first humans living in North America migrated from Asia over a prehistoric land connection near the present Bering Strait between Alaska and Russia.

Constructed Response

Why are the indigenous people of North America referred to as "Indians?" Use at least two details from the selection to support your answer.

_____

_____

_____

_____

_____

Name: _____ Date: _____

Explore: People of North America Bookmark

Directions: Research one of the indigenous peoples of North America. Using this information, fill in the blanks on the bookmark. On the other side of the bookmark, create an illustration that represents the culture. Cut out the bookmark. Punch a hole at the top, run yarn through the hole, and tie. For a sturdier bookmark, copy the bookmark image onto heavier cardstock.

Nationality:

_____

Holidays or Special Celebrations:

_____

_____

_____

_____

Foods:

_____

_____

_____

_____

Etiquette and Customs:

_____

_____

_____

_____

Name:

_____

Canada: Close-Up

Both French and English explorers and settlers came to what is now known as Canada in the late seventeenth century. The British gained control when they captured the French city of Quebec in 1759. In 1931, Canada was declared to be a self-governing **dominion** within the British Empire. Today, it is a **constitutional monarchy**, with a parliamentary system of government. This means that the king or queen of England is the official head of state. However, elected members of Parliament run the country. A prime minister heads the government. The **prime minister** is the head of the political party that has the majority of members in the House of Commons, which is one of the two houses of Parliament.

Canada has ten **provinces** and three **territories**. The provinces are political divisions, much like states in the United States. The territories have more limited government, since so few people live there.

Provinces
- The eastern provinces include: Newfoundland, Nova Scotia, Prince Edward Island, and New Brunswick. Fishing is a major industry in these provinces. Other industries include mining, forestry, and tourism.
- **Quebec** is Canada's largest province. Four out of five residents of Quebec speak French; **French** was declared the official language of Quebec in 1974. Many of Quebec's citizens want the province to separate from Canada and form its own country.
- The central provinces are Ontario, Manitoba, Saskatchewan, and Alberta. Agriculture is a major industry in this region. Farmers raise cattle and a variety of crops. Industry and oil production have increased in the region in recent years.
- British Columbia is Canada's most western province. The **Rocky Mountains** cover most of British Columbia's land. **Vancouver**, in British Columbia, is Canada's major port on the Pacific Ocean.

Territories
- Canada's three territories are the Northwest Territories, the Yukon Territory, and Nunavut. These territories are mostly tundra, which has poor soil and a cold climate but is rich in mineral deposits. Nunavut separated from part of the Northwest Territories in 1999; it is home to many of the **Inuit**, who are also known as Eskimos.

Canada and the United States share a 4,000-mile border. It is the world's longest **unfortified** border. The two nations are major trading partners. Trade with Canada is about 20 percent of the total of U.S. **exports**. Canada's trade with the United States is about 74 percent of its **imports** and 86 percent of its exports.

The Great Lakes and the St. Lawrence Seaway make up Canada's most important waterway. Completed in 1959, the Seaway allowed Montreal and Toronto to become ports for ocean-going **vessels**.

Name: _____ Date: _____

Knowledge Check

Matching

_____ 1. Inuit

_____ 2. Quebec

_____ 3. Vancouver

_____ 4. French

_____ 5. Rocky Mountains

a. official language of Quebec

b. major port on the Pacific Ocean

c. cover most of British Columbia's land

d. also known as Eskimos

e. Canada's largest province

Multiple Choice

6. How many provinces does Canada have?

    a. 3

    b. 7

    c. 5

    d. 10

7. This is Canada's most western province.

    a. British Columbia

    b. Quebec

    c. Newfoundland

    d. Nova Scotia

Did You Know?

Canada has hosted the Olympics three times: the Summer Games in Montreal (1976); the Winter Games in Calgary (1988) and Vancouver (2010).

Constructed Response

Canada is a constitutional monarchy. Explain how this type of government works. Use details from the reading selection to support your answer.

_____

_____

_____

_____

_____

_____

_____

_____

_____

Name: _____ Date: _____

Map Follow-Up

Directions: Match the numbers on the map with the provinces and territories of Canada.

_____ Northwest Territories   _____ New Brunswick   _____ Nova Scotia

_____ Yukon Territory   _____ British Columbia   _____ Alberta

_____ Saskatchewan   _____ Manitoba   _____ Nunavut

_____ Prince Edward Island   _____ Quebec   _____ Ontario

_____ Newfoundland and Labrador

Canada

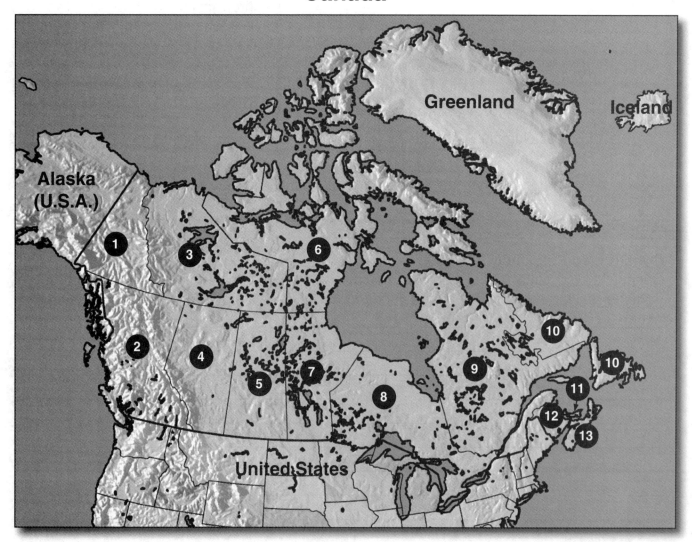

The United States: Close-Up

The United States consists of 50 states. The first 48 states make up what is often referred to as the **continental United States**. Alaska and Hawaii are not connected by land to the other states.

The population of the United States is over 308 million. Eighty-two percent of the population lives in **urban** areas. New York City, Los Angeles, and Chicago are the three largest cities in the United States.

Geographical Facts

*   Alaska contains much tundra and has a subarctic climate. The Hawaiian Islands are the tops of volcanoes in the Pacific Ocean and have a mild, almost tropical climate.

*   The continental states have three major regions. The eastern coastal area and the Appalachian Mountains were the earliest to be settled. The Great Plains stretch from the Appalachian Mountains in the east to the Rocky Mountains in the west. The Rocky Mountains, the Cascades Range, and the Sierra Nevadas divide the plains from the western coastal area.

*   The highest point in the United States is **Mount McKinley** in Alaska (20,320 feet; 6,194 m), and its lowest point is **Death Valley** in California (282 feet [86 m] below sea level). The highest point in the continental United States is **Mount Whitney** in California (14,494 feet [4,418 m] above sea level).

*   The Missouri, Mississippi, and Red Rivers form the nation's major waterways and drain most of the central two-thirds of the land. The rivers have a combined length of 3,710 miles (5,971 km). The **Mississippi** is the longest river in the United States at 2,348 miles (3,778 km). The United States has many notable lakes, including the Great Lakes, as well as the Great Salt Lake in Utah.

History Overview

The first European explorers included the Spanish under the leadership of Ponce de Leon and Hernando de Soto. They explored the southern and southeastern regions. Early French explorers included Jacques Cartier and Samuel de Champlain. Many early French settlers were fur trappers and traders. The first English settlement was in 1607. Eventually, the English gained control of most of the land, and the American colonies were ruled by England until the Revolutionary War.

From the time of its independence, the United States continued its westward **expansion**. It was rich in resources and soon became a leading manufacturing nation. The United States had not been very active in world events until after the Spanish-American War in the 1890s; however, after the war, America continued to grow as a major world power and industrial nation.

After World War II, the United States led world trade. As other nations recovered from the war and rebuilt their economies, they competed more with American trade. In the 1980s, United States **imports** from other countries exceeded its **exports** for the first time. Today, it continues to import more than it exports.

Name: _____ Date: _____

Knowledge Check

Matching

_____ 1. Mississippi

_____ 2. Mount Whitney

_____ 3. Mount McKinley

_____ 4. Death Valley

_____ 5. continental United States

a. the highest point in the United States

b. highest point in the continental United States

c. lowest point in the United States

d. first 48 states

e. the longest river in the United States

Multiple Choice

6. When was the first English settlement established in North America?

    a. 1980

    b. 1607

    c. 1890

    d. 1542

7. What is the population of the United States?

    a. over 308 million

    b. under 2 million

    c. over 140 billion

    d. under 30 million

Did You Know?

The Great Salt Lake is saltier than the oceans because the rate of evaporation exceeds its supply of water.

Constructed Response

Explain why there is such an extreme difference between the climates of Alaska and Hawaii. Use details from the reading selection to support your answer.

_____

_____

_____

_____

_____

_____

Name: _____ Date: _____

Map Follow-Up

Directions: The eight major mountain ranges of North America are listed below. Draw and label the mountain ranges on the map. Use an atlas to help locate the mountain ranges.

Alaska Range	Appalachian Mountains	Brooks Range
Cascades	Coastal Ranges	Rocky Mountains
Sierra Madres	Sierra Nevada	

Mountain Ranges of the United States

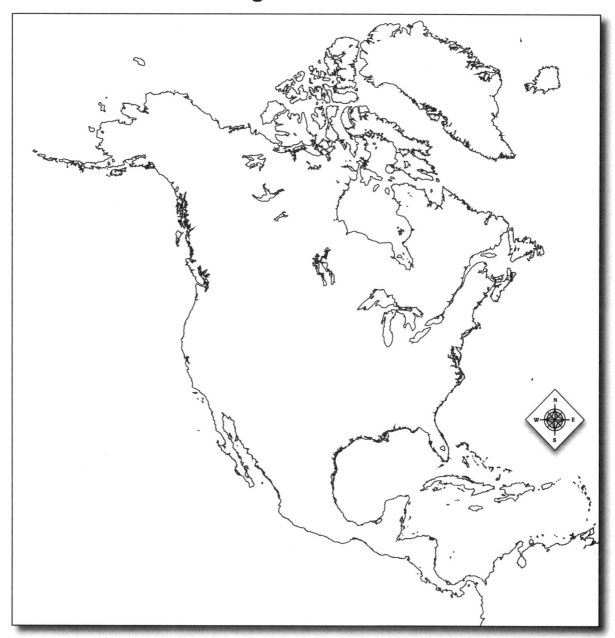

Name: _____ Date: _____

Map Follow-Up

Directions: Ten major rivers of the United States are numbered on the map below. Match the number on the map with the name of the river. Use an atlas if you need help.

____ Colorado River

____ Mississippi River

____ Red River

____ Tennessee River

____ Columbia River

____ Missouri River

____ Rio Grande River

____ Illinois River

____ Ohio River

____ Snake River

Major Rivers of the United States

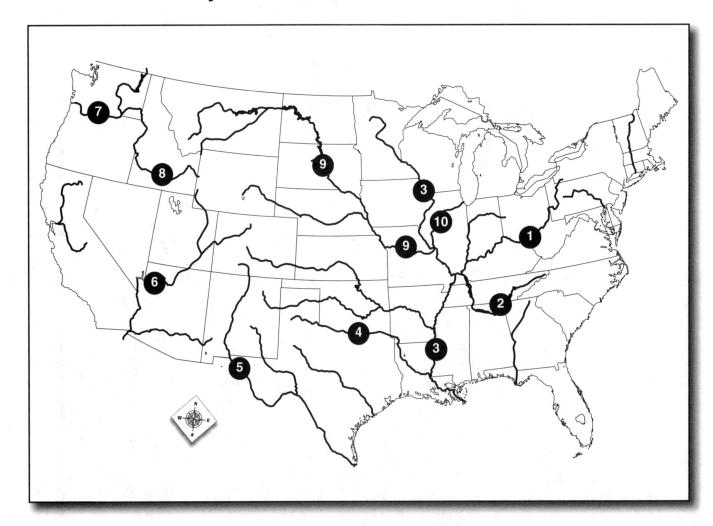

Mexico: Close-Up

The official name of Mexico is **The United Mexican States**. In Spanish, it is ***Los Estados Unidos Mexicanos***.

Geography

- Mexico shares a 1,933-mile (3,111-km) border with the United States. To the south, Mexico shares its border with Guatemala and Belize. Its western coast is on the Pacific Ocean, and the eastern coast is on the Gulf of Mexico.

- Climate and geography vary in Mexico. It is a mountainous country with two mountain ranges enclosing a dry **plateau**. Mexico also contains large deserts, beautiful sand beaches, and jungle **wetlands**.

- Many mineral resources are found in Mexico, but there is limited farmland. Major crops include citrus fruits, beans, corn, bananas, pineapple, cotton, coffee, sugar cane, cacao, coca, wheat, oats, and rice.

- Mexico's major industries include **petroleum** and tourism. It may have the largest oil reserve in the Western Hemisphere, but most of the oil is difficult to get to and has not been developed. Auto plants and steel mills are increasing production after the recent global economic recession.

Facts of Interest

Mexico is the largest Spanish-speaking country in the world. It is the second-largest Roman Catholic nation in the world.

There is a colorful **diversity** in Mexico's culture. The major blend is of Spanish and Native American culture. Ancient civilizations included the Mayan, Olmec, Toltec, and Aztec Native American cultures. The Spanish **conquest** began in the sixteenth century and lasted for over 300 years.

Mexico is a nation of contrast. It has ruins of ancient cities, churches from the Spanish colonial period, and modern skyscrapers. Colorful **fiestas**, or celebrations, are part of Mexico's culture. Popular entertainment includes bullfights, soccer games, and rodeos. In addition to national holidays, Mexicans observe most Roman Catholic religious celebrations.

Mexico went through a period of fast-growing population up until the 1990s. Some of its people live in great wealth just a few miles from some of the world's largest slums. The **unemployment** rate continues to grow each year. **Mexico City** is the capital of Mexico. The population of the Mexico City region is the third-largest urban area in the world. Increasing pollution, crime, and illegal drug usage and sales plague the country.

Mexico has many popular tourist sites. In addition to the ancient Native American ruins, thousands of tourists visit Mexico's resort cities. Popular vacation resort **destinations** include Cancún, Acapulco, Mazatlán, Puerto Vallarta, and Veracruz.

Name: _____ Date: _____

Knowledge Check

Matching

____ 1. Mexico   a. Mexico's capital
____ 2. The United Mexican States   b. official name of Mexico in Spanish
____ 3. *Estados Unidos Mexicanos*   c. celebrations
____ 4. Mexico City   d. largest Spanish-speaking country in the world
____ 5. fiestas   e. official name of Mexico

Multiple Choice

6. How long is the border between Mexico and the United States?

   a. 1,933 miles
   b. 3,000 miles
   c. 1,000 miles
   d. 3,933 miles

7. Which is NOT a popular entertainment in Mexico?

   a. bullfights
   b. soccer games
   c. rodeos
   d. snowboarding

Did You Know?

September 16 is Mexico's Independence Day. It celebrates Mexico's 1810 rebellion against Spanish control. Miguel Hidalgo led the first group to rebel and is called the "Father of the Nation."

Constructed Response

Explain why having a fast-growing population led to problems for Mexico. Use details from the reading selection to support your answer.

_____
_____
_____
_____
_____
_____
_____

Name: _____ Date: _____

Map Follow-Up

Directions: Match the names of the nations, oceans, and regions with the numbers on the map.

_____ Atlantic Ocean   _____ Central America   _____ Gulf of California

_____ Mexico City   _____ United States   _____ Pacific Ocean

_____ South America   _____ Mexico   _____ West Indies Islands

_____ Baja California   _____ Yucatan Peninsula   _____ Gulf of Mexico

Mexico and Its Neighbors

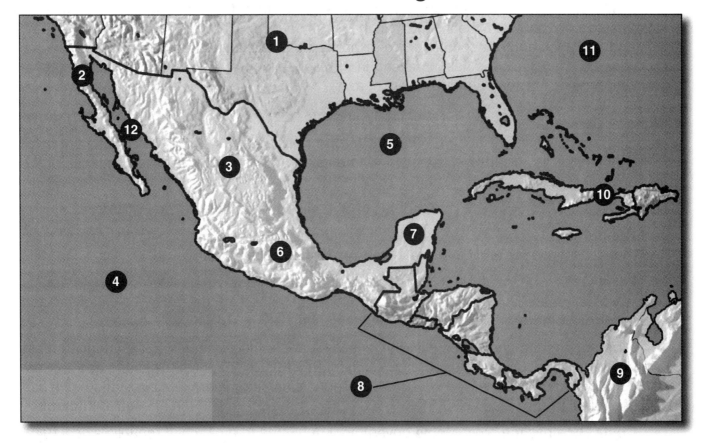

Central America: Close-Up

Seven nations make up the region known as Central America. Each of the Central American countries is unique. Spanish is the major language of all of the Central American nations except Belize, which adopted English as its official language. Most Costa Ricans have European ancestors. Most people of El Salvador, Honduras, and Nicaragua are mestizo, or **descendants** of mixed native and Spanish backgrounds. Many citizens of Belize and Panama are of African descent.

Agriculture is the major industry in the region. Bananas, coffee, cotton, rice, and sugar are all major exports. Ranchers raise sheep for wool and cattle for beef.

Fishing, mining, and forestry are other important industries. Pine, rosewood, and mahogany are harvested for exporting. Minerals found in the region include coal, copper, gold, iron ore, lead, nickel, and zinc. Fish and seafood caught for export include anchovies, lobster, shrimp, and tuna. The number of small factories has increased in the last several years, and tourism continues to grow in importance to Central America's economy.

Nations of Central America

- **Guatemala** was the site of the **ancient** Mayan civilization. In recent years, constant fighting has hurt its **economy**. Foreign investments and tourism have declined because of the political situation.

- **Belize** was known as British Honduras until it gained its independence in 1981.

- **Honduras** is Central America's least-developed nation. Unrest among its neighbors, Nicaragua, El Salvador, and Guatemala, constantly threatens Honduras' peace.

- **El Salvador** is Central America's smallest and most **densely** populated nation. For many years, only a few families owned the land. Unfortunately, the recent redistribution of the land has brought **controversy** and unrest in the nation.

- **Nicaragua** is the poorest country in Central America and continues to experience unrest as the military fights with opposition soldiers. Protests over corrupt elections and against current leaders often lead to violence. Nicaragua also struggles with a population increase of about 2 percent each year, making it difficult for the country to remain **self-sufficient**.

- **Costa Rica** has the most **stable** government. It has been a peaceful republic since 1949. This has allowed it to have Central America's highest standard of living, **literacy** rate, and life expectancy.

- **Panama** is famous for the canal that opened in 1914. The Panama Canal connects the Atlantic and Pacific Oceans, saving a long voyage around South America.

Name: _____ Date: _____

Knowledge Check

Matching

_____ 1. El Salvador

_____ 2. Belize

_____ 3. Guatemala

_____ 4. Panama

_____ 5. Honduras

a. was the site of the ancient Mayan civilization

b. famous for the canal that opened in 1914

c. Central America's least-developed nation

d. was known as British Honduras

e. Central America's smallest and most densely populated nation

Multiple Choice

6. What is Belize's official language?
   a. Spanish
   b. English
   c. French
   d. German

7. Which Central American country has the most stable government?

   a. Belize
   b. Honduras
   c. Costa Rica
   d. Nicaragua

Did You Know?

Chicle, a sap from the sapodilla tree grown in Guatemala and Belize, is used to make chewing gum.

Constructed Response

Explain how the problems facing individual countries of Central America affect the economy of the region. Use details from the selection to support your answer.

_____

_____

_____

_____

_____

_____

_____

Name: _____ Date: _____

Map Follow-Up

Directions: Match the names below with the numbers on the map.

_____ Atlantic Ocean   _____ Pacific Ocean   _____ Nicaragua

_____ El Salvador   _____ Honduras   _____ Gulf of Mexico

_____ Caribbean Sea   _____ Panama   _____ Belize

_____ Guatemala   _____ Costa Rica

Nations of Central America

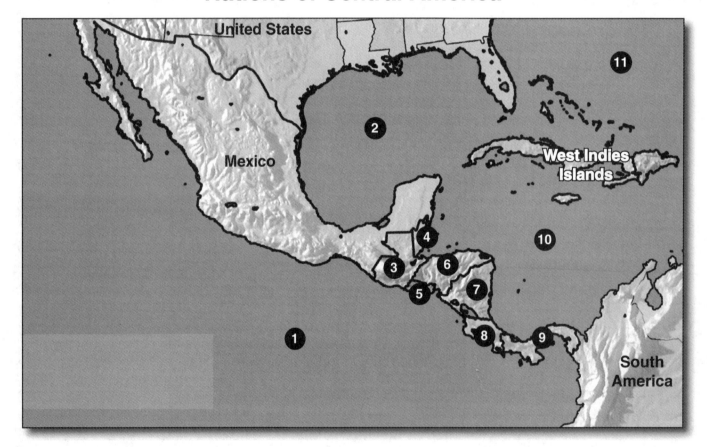

North America's Islands: Close-Up

The continent of North America has hundreds of islands off its coasts. Most of the islands, such as Canada's Prince Edward Island and Vancouver Island, and the United States' islands of Manhattan and the Florida Keys, are part of each nearby country. Other islands, such as Greenland and the Caribbean Islands, are independent nations. The Caribbean Islands are also referred to as the West Indies. They include the Bahamas, the Greater Antilles, and the Lesser Antilles.

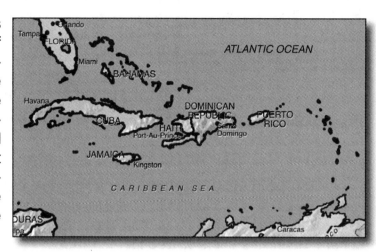

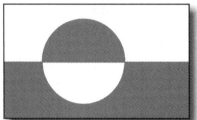

The West Indies

Greenland is the world's largest island. Located in the North Atlantic Ocean, it is about one-third the size of the continental United States. It is a self-governing part of Denmark. Sheet glaciers, called **ice caps**, cover over 80 percent of Greenland. The island's population is about 57,000, which includes a large Eskimo population.

The **Bahamas** are a group of over 700 islands. Only 22 of these islands are inhabited. Even though they are in the Atlantic Ocean, they are often referred to as Caribbean islands. The Bahamas are an independent member of the British Commonwealth. The capital of the Bahamas, Nassau, is a popular tourist destination. Tourism is the major industry. Over two-thirds of the population is involved in the tourist industry. Christopher Columbus probably landed on one of the Bahamas, San Salvador, in 1492.

The **Greater Antilles** include the islands of Cuba, Hispaniola (Haiti and the Dominican Republic), Jamaica, and Puerto Rico, located across the northern edge of the Caribbean Sea.

Cuba is the largest and most **populous** of all of the West Indies. Christopher Columbus visited in 1492, and the Spanish began controlling the island in 1511. Cuba remained under Spanish control until the Spanish-American War in 1898. It then came under U.S. protection. In 1958, a revolution put a Communist government into power under the leadership of Fidel Castor. Havana, its capital, is only 92 **nautical miles** (170 km) from Florida. Agriculture is Cuba's major industry. Important crops include sugar cane and tobacco. Tourism is also a major industry.

Puerto Rico is another popular tourist destination. Agriculture was the major industry until the mid-1950s, when factories became more plentiful. Major crops include sugar cane, tobacco, and coffee. In 1952, Puerto Rico became a commonwealth with an association with the United States. Puerto Ricans are United States citizens. Occasionally, groups of citizens promote Puerto Rico to become the fifty-first state of the United States.

Hispaniola: The Dominican Republic and Haiti share an island named Hispaniola; however, the two countries have little in common. Christopher Columbus landed on this island in 1492.

The **Dominican Republic** has a Hispanic **culture**, and most of its population is of Spanish or mixed Spanish and African ancestry. Its capital, Santo Domingo, is the oldest city in the Western Hemisphere. Spanish settlers arrived there in 1496.

Haiti has had a strong French influence in its culture. Most of its people are of African and French descent. Haiti is the poorest country in the Western Hemisphere. In January 2010, a magnitude 7.0 earthquake destroyed much of the area in and around Haiti's capital Port-au-Prince. Reports of the death toll range from 92,000 to 316,000, with as many as 1.8 million people left homeless.

Jamaica is a mountainous island. Christopher Columbus visited the island during his 1494 voyage. It came under Spanish rule until the British took control in 1655. It then became an independent part of the British Commonwealth in 1962. For many years, plantation owners brought over African slaves to work in the sugar cane and coffee fields. Agriculture is still an important part of Jamaica's **economy**, but today, the island's major industry is tourism.

The **Lesser Antilles** are the smaller islands located in a curve around the eastern edge of the Caribbean Sea. The Virgin Islands are part of the Lesser Antilles.

The **Virgin Islands** are divided into the British Virgin Islands and the United States Virgin Islands. The British Virgin Islands include 36 islands. They have a total land area of 59 square miles (153 sq. km). The U.S. Virgin Islands include 50 islands. They have 136 square miles (352 sq. km). St. Croix, St. Thomas, and St. John are three of the largest islands. The United States purchased the U.S. Virgin Islands from Denmark in 1917.

The islands have a mild climate and beautiful scenery. Tourism is the major industry in the islands. Many of the islands' people make craft items to sell to the tourists. Because there is duty-free and sales-tax-free shopping, tourists buy imported goods from around the world in Virgin Island cities. Electronics, jewelry, liquor, tobacco, and textile products are some of the major items sold in the U.S. Virgin Islands.

Name: _____ Date: _____

Knowledge Check

Matching

____ 1. Cuba
____ 2. ice caps
____ 3. Caribbean Islands
____ 4. Greenland
____ 5. Bahamas

a. referred to as the West Indies
b. a group of over 700 islands
c. sheet glaciers
d. largest and most populous of all of the West Indies
e. the world's largest island

Multiple Choice

6. What is the capital of Cuba?

   a. Havana
   b. Dominican Republic
   c. Haiti
   d. Nassau

7. What is the capital of the Dominican Republic?

   a. Santo Domingo
   b. Havana
   c. Nassau
   d. Jamaica

Did You Know?

The West Indies islands are actually the tops of a mountain range. They separate the Atlantic Ocean from the Caribbean Sea.

Constructed Response

In your opinion, which of North America's islands would make the best vacation destination? Use details from the reading selection to support your answer.

_____

_____

_____

_____

_____

_____

_____

Name: _____ Date: _____

Map Follow-Up

Directions: Match the names below with the numbers on the map.

____ Atlantic Ocean   ____ Bahamas   ____ Caribbean Sea

____ Cuba   ____ Haiti   ____ Dominican Republic

____ Gulf of Mexico   ____ Jamaica   ____ Puerto Rico

____ Virgin Islands

The Nations of the Caribbean

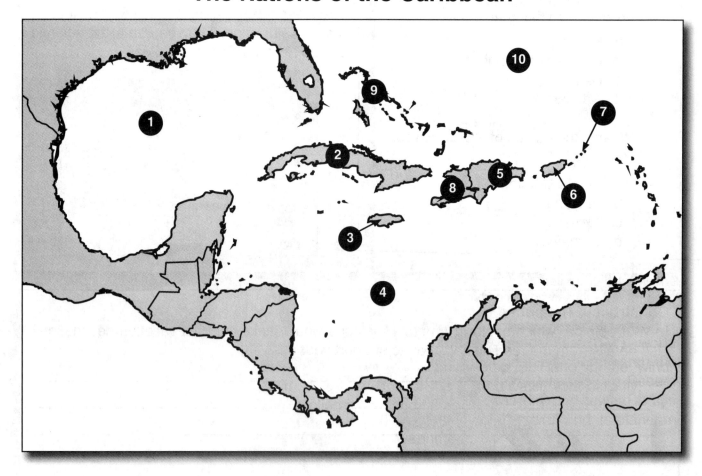

Glossary

agricultural – relating to farming

ancestry – line of descent

ancient – very old; an early period of history

arctic – region around the north pole

Bahamas – a group of over 700 islands

bordered – touching the edge or boundary

Canadian Shield – region that includes eastern Canada, most of Greenland, and part of the northern United States

central plain – extends from southern Canada to Texas; also known as the Great Plains

crude oil – oil that has not been processed

coal – a type of rock containing carbon that is mined and burned for fuel

coastal plain – region that covers most of the eastern United States and Mexico

conquest – the act of conquering or taking over by war

conservationists – people who protect natural resources

constitutional monarchy – parliamentary system of government

consume – use

continent – a large landmass completely or mostly surrounded by water

Continental Drift - Alfred Lothar Wegener's theory that the large landmass Pangaea had broken up and the continents were made of lighter rock that floated on top of heavier rock

continental United States – the first 48 states of the United States

controversy – something that causes argument

culture – a social group's customs and beliefs

Death Valley – lowest point in the United States

decreased – lessened or reduced

densely – tightly packed

descendants – those who come from an original person or group

descent – originating from ancestors

destinations – journeys

diverse – different

diversity – a condition of being different

domesticated – tamed

dominion – self-governing nation

economy – activities related to the production and distribution of goods and services in a particular geographic region

expansion – increasing

export – send to some other country

extinct – no more living members of a species

fiestas – celebrations

fishing – catching fish and other seafood

forestry – science of forest care

Gondwanaland – the name of the lower part of Pangaea when it divided into two continents during the Triassic Age

Greater Antilles – the larger islands across the northern edge of the Caribbean Sea

Greenland – the world's largest island

habitat – the place in an ecosystem where an organism lives

highland climate – the climate in mountain regions; has mild winters, warm summers, and significant amounts of precipitation

Hispaniola – island in the Caribbean that includes the Dominican Republic and Haiti

humid continental – regions with cold winters and hot summers, with adequate amounts of precipitation

humid subtropical – regions where the winters are often warm and the summers are hot and humid

ice caps – sheet glaciers

import – to bring from another country

indigenous – one who originally lived in a certain location

industries – businesses

inhabitant – one that occupies a particular region

Inuit – natives of Alaska and Canada; Eskimos

Isthmus of Panama – a narrow strip of land that connects North and South America

Laurasia – the name of the upper part of Pangaea when it divided into two continents during the Triassic Age

Lesser Antilles – the smaller islands located in a curve around the eastern edge of the Caribbean Sea

literacy – the ability to read and write

major – most important

majority – most

marine west coast climate – regions that are very humid with much precipitation and mild temperatures

Mediterranean climate – regions with hot, dry, sunny summers and a winter rainy season

mestizo – a person of mixed Native American and European (mostly Spanish) descent

Mexico's climate zone – contains desert and semi-desert regions as well as some highland and tropical areas

Mississippi River – longest river in the United States

Mount McKinley – highest point in the United States

Mount Whitney – highest point in the continental United States

natural resources – materials from the environment

nautical miles – sea distance

official – formal

Pangaea – ancient landmass believed to have broken up to form today's continents

pesticides – chemicals used to destroy pests (bugs)

petroleum – oil

Glossary (cont.)

plateau – usually extensive land area having a relatively level surface raised sharply above adjacent land on at least one side

plates – giant slabs of the earth's crust

Plate Tectonics – theory suggesting that plates move a few inches each year

populous – densely populated

provinces – divisions of a country

primary – first or most important

prime minister – head of the government; leader of the majority party

Quebec – Canada's largest province

region – an area of the world

self-sufficient – able to provide for oneself

semi-desert – regions with hot daytime temperatures with cool nights and very little rainfall

species – a group of organisms that can mate and produce offspring that in turn can produce more offspring

stable – steady; not changing

subarctic – regions immediately outside the arctic region with similar climate conditions

territories – subdivision of a country

tropical climate zone – regions with hot temperatures and much rainfall throughout the year

unemployment – being without a job

unfortified – not secured

United Mexican States – official name of Mexico; *Los Estados Unidos Mexicanos* in Spanish

urban – city

Vancouver – Canada's major port on the Pacific Ocean

vessels – boats

Western Hemisphere – the land of South America and North America

wetlands – regions containing a great deal of soil moisture; for example, a swamp

Bibliography

Individual Books:

Bock, Judy and Rachel Krauz. *Scholastic Encyclopedia of the United States.* Scholastic Reference, 1997.

Curlee, Lynn. *Into the Ice, The Story of Arctic Exploration.* Houghton Mifflin, 1998.

Hermandez, Romel. *Caribbean Islands: Facts & Figures.* Mason Crest Publishers, 2008.

Kramme, Michael. *Mexico.* Mark Twain Media/Carson-Dellosa Publishing LLC, 1999.

Hudson, John C. *Across this Land: a Regional Geography of the United States and Canada.* Johns Hopkins University Press, 2002.

Mattern, Joanne. *Animal Geography: North America.* Perfection Learning, 2001

McKnight, Tom Lee. *Regional Geography of the United States and Canada.* Prentice Hall, 2004.

Series:

Cultures of the World (Series published by Benchmark Books/Marshall Cavendish Children's Books). Each book was published between 1998 and 2011, contains 128 pages. Countries included: *Bahamas, Belize, Canada, Costa Rica, Cuba, Dominican Republic, El Salvador, Guatemala, Haiti, Honduras, Jamaica, Panama, Puerto Rico,* and *Nicaragua*

Major World Nations (Series published by Chelsea House). Each book was published between 1997 and 2001, page counts vary. Countries included: *Bahamas, Canada, Cuba, Dominican Republic, El Salvador, Guatemala, Haiti, Honduras, Jamaica, Nicaragua, Panama,* and *Puerto Rico*

Enchantment of the World (Series published by Children's Press). Each book was published between 1997 and 2008, contains 144 pages. Countries included: *Bahamas, Canada, Costa Rica, Cuba, Dominican Republic, El Salvador, Greenland, Guatemala, Honduras, Mexico, Nicaragua,* and *Panama*

Answer Keys

The Continents
Knowledge Check (p. 4)
Matching
1. c   2. d   3. e   4. a   5. b
Multiple Choice
6. b   7. a
Constructed Response
The earth's crust consists of about 20 plates. Plate Tectonics suggest that these plates move a few inches each year. When Pangaea broke up, the continents on the plates moved apart.
Map Follow-Up (p. 5)
1. North America   2. South America   3. Europe
4. Africa   5. Antarctica   6. Asia
7. Australia   8. Arctic Ocean   9. Atlantic Ocean
10. Indian Ocean   11. Pacific Ocean

The Continent of North America
Knowledge Check (p. 9)
Matching
1. b   2. c   3. d   4. a   5. e
Multiple Choice
6. c   7. d
Constructed Response
The coastal plain covers most of the eastern United States and Mexico. The central plain extends from southern Canada to Texas. The central plain has most of the continent's agricultural lands.
Map Follow-Up (p. 10)
1. Greenland   2. Canada   3. United States
4. West Indies Islands   5. Mexico
6. Central America
Teacher check bodies of water.

North America's Climate
Knowledge Check (p. 12)
Matching
1. b   2. c   3. a   4. e   5. d
Multiple Choice
6. a   7. d
Constructed Response
Answers will vary from state to state.
Map Follow-Up (p. 13)
Teacher check map.

North America's Resources and Industries
Knowledge Check (p. 15)
Matching
1. e   2. d   3. a   4. c   5. b
Multiple Choice
6. c   7. d

Constructed Response
Natural resources allow a country to develop industries. Many of the products can be exported. The more a country exports, the more the country's wealth grows.
Map Follow-Up (p. 16)
Teacher check map.

North America's Animal Life
Knowledge Check (p. 18)
Matching
1. e   2. d   3. b   4. a   5. c
Multiple Choice
6. a   7. d
Constructed Response
As humans settled, natural habitats of most animals decreased. Also, pollution and the use of pesticides helped decrease the animal populations.

The Native People of North America
Knowledge Check (p. 21)
Matching
1. c   2. e   3. a   4. b   5. d
Multiple Choice
6. c   7. b
Constructed Response
It is believed that approximately 20,000 to 30,000 years ago, hunters looking for new hunting grounds crossed a land bridge that connected Asia and North America. The land bridge, which no longer exists, was near what is now the Bering Strait.
Map Follow-Up (p. 22)
1. Pacific Northwest   2. California   3. Plateau
4. Great Basin   5. Pueblo   6. Plains
7. Woodland   8. Southeast
9. Northern Hunters

The People of North America
Knowledge Check (p. 24)
Matching
1. c   2. d   3. e   4. a   5. b
Multiple Choice
6. b   7. c
Constructed Response
The term Indian has its origin from Christopher Columbus. Upon landing in the Americas, he thought he was in the East Indies islands.

Canada
Knowledge Check (p. 27)
Matching
1. d 2. e 3. b 4. a 5. c
Multiple Choice
6. d 7. a
Constructed Response
This means that the king or queen of England is the official head of state. However, elected members of Parliament run the country. A prime minister heads the government. The prime minister is the head of the political party that has the majority of members in the House of Commons, which is one of the two houses of Parliament.
Map Follow-Up (p. 28)
1. Yukon Territory
2. British Columbia
3. Northwest Territories
4. Alberta
5. Saskatchewan
6. Nunavut Territory
7. Manitoba
8. Ontario
9. Quebec
10. Newfoundland and Labrador
11. Prince Edward Island
12. New Brunswick
13. Nova Scotia

The United States
Knowledge Check (p. 30)
Matching
1. e 2. b 3. a 4. c 5. d
Multiple Choice
6. b 7. a
Constructed Response
Alaska contains a great deal of tundra and has a sub-arctic climate. Alaska is the farthest northern state. The Hawaiian Islands are the tops of volcanoes in the Pacific Ocean and have a mild, tropical climate. Hawaii lies near the equator.
Map Follow-Up: Mountain Ranges (p. 31)
Teacher check map.
Map Follow-Up: Rivers (p. 32)
1. Ohio River
2. Tennessee River
3. Mississippi River
4. Red River
5. Rio Grande River
6. Colorado River
7. Columbia River
8. Snake River
9. Missouri River
10. Illinois River

Mexico
Knowledge Check (p. 34)
Matching
1. d 2. e 3. b 4. a 5. c
Multiple Choice
6. a 7. d
Constructed Response
Many people live in slums. The unemployment rate continues to grow. Pollution, crime, and illegal drug use and sales increase.

Map Follow-Up (p. 35)
1. United States
2. Baja California
3. Mexico
4. Pacific Ocean
5. Gulf of Mexico
6. Mexico City
7. Yucatan Peninsula
8. Central America
9. South America
10. West Indies
11. Atlantic Ocean
12. Gulf of California

Central America
Knowledge Check (p. 37)
Matching
1. e 2. d 3. a 4. b 5. c
Multiple Choice
6. b 7. c
Constructed Response
Political unrest, violence, and poverty make it hard for countries to be self-sufficient. Foreign investments and tourism have declined because of unstable political situations.
Map Follow-Up (p. 38)
1. Pacific Ocean
2. Gulf of Mexico
3. Guatemala
4. Belize
5. El Salvador
6. Honduras
7. Nicaragua
8. Costa Rica
9. Panama
10. Caribbean Sea
11. Atlantic Ocean

North America's Islands
Knowledge Check (p. 41)
Matching
1. d 2. c 3. a 4. e 5. b
Multiple Choice
6. a 7. a
Constructed Response
Answers will vary.
Map Follow-Up (p. 42)
1. Gulf of Mexico
2. Cuba
3. Jamaica
4. Caribbean Sea
5. Dominican Republic
6. Puerto Rico
7. Virgin Islands
8. Haiti
9. Bahamas
10. Atlantic Ocean